Mother of the Year!

Crazy, Funny and True Advice from Moms Telling It Like It Is!

🗲 WILLOW CREEK PRESS®

© 2013 Working Girls Design

All Rights reserved. No part of this book may be reproduced or transmitted in any form by any means, electronic or mechanical, including photocopying, recording, or by any information storage and retrieval system, without written permission from the Publisher.

Published by Willow Creek Press, Inc.
P.O. Box 147, Minocqua, Wisconsin 54548

Printed in China

To:

From:

ON ACCESSORIES:

It's important to keep your jewelry and accessories forever. Your clothes will judge you, you'll love them when you feel skinny and hate them when you don't. But your accessories, they never judge.

———

Jillian's Mom
Age 45

ON BAD MOODS:

Sometimes men get in a
surly mood for no good reason.
Just leave him at home
with the tv remote and
go make yourself happy.
That's basically why
malls were invented.

———

Marcia's Mom
Age 61

ON BEING AUTHENTIC:

Just tell him you don't like watching all-star wrestling. Pretending that you do, well that's like driving 800 miles to go clothes shopping at K-mart. It just doesn't make sense, does it?

Angelica's Mom
Age 46

ON BORROWING MONEY:

You want to borrow some money? Here's a plan, why don't I loan you the money and you can use that to pay back the money you already owe me.

———

Brooke's Mom
Age 44

ON BREAKUPS:

Oh sweetheart,
men are like trains, if
you miss one, another
one will be coming
along shortly.

———

Ava's Mom
Age 56

ON CHILDBIRTH:

Does it hurt? I'm not going to lie, take all the pain you've ever felt and times it by infinity and then, you are halfway there.

———

Amber's Mom
Age 48

ON CHOCOLATE:

I do want you to eat healthy, but there will be certain times of the month where it's perfectly okay to say, screw the vegetables, I want chocolate.

Lois's Mom
Age 52

ON CREDIT CARDS:

I know you think you really
need those $200 jeans,
but trust me in 3 years when
you can't get your left thigh
in the waistline and you've paid
$150 in finance charges,
you're gonna hate yourself.

———

Megan's Mom
Age 62

ON DIETING:

You could try dieting, but you know there's probably a reason Spanx is a billion-dollar business. Sometimes it's just easier to throw some cash at the problem and be done with it.

Jana's Mom
Age 51

ON EXERCISE:

It's important to exercise. It's not important to me because your dad would hump a potato sack, but you are single, it should be important to you.

Siena's Mom
Age 52

ON FALLING IN LOVE:

It's great you found someone you love, but does he love you more than you love him? It's never good to be the needy one dear.

Lauren's Mom
Age 47

ON FINDING LOVE:

I know you think the most important love in the world is going to come from a man, but it's not true. The best love is when you can learn to love yourself as much as your shoe collection.

———

Chris's Mom
Age 49

ON FOLLOWING INSTRUCTIONS:

No, you can't have your teeth whitened. I paid $600 for a retainer you hardly wore. I guess now you get to have crooked and yellow teeth.

Juliana's Mom
Age 46

ON GRANDCHILDREN:

I never felt the need to spoil you. I didn't want to undermine your development. But my grandchildren, well that's another story. It's payback time.

———

Joselyn's Mom
Age 56

ON GROWING OLDER:

One day you're going to look in the mirror and see all these wrinkles and think to yourself, "oh crap." Don't worry, that feeling goes away because your eyesight gets worse and you don't notice as much.

Marianne's Mom
Age 78

ON HARD WORK:

You got on prom court, that's great, now get your math grades up or in 2 years your greatest accomplishment will be fast-food worker of the month.

———

Shari's Mom
Age 52

ON HOUSEWORK:

It's fine to do it, just don't do it all. Because believe me, those men will let you do it all.

Kelly's Mom
Age 46

When I said I do, I didn't mean Everything!

If you need me I'll be on my pedestal.

ON HOW TO BE TREATED:

Any man who tells you that you're spoiled or that you don't deserve to be pampered is either not very bright or not very nice. And you want a man who is nice and bright.

———

Juliana's Mom
Age 46

ON LEARNING TO DRIVE:

I didn't say you were a remarkable driver. I said the way you totaled both of our cars without ever leaving the driveway was remarkable.

Jillian's Mom
Age 46

I don't know were I'm going, but I bet I get there

Faster

I don't expect everything handed to me, just put it down anywhere.

ON LIFE:

You don't like the casserole? Well I don't like having fat thighs and ingrates for offspring, but sometimes that's what life deals you.

Candice's Mom
Age 29

ON LOVING YOUR SISTER:

I don't like her attitude either sometimes, but I birthed you both, so hug it out. I need to keep this big, happy family fantasy intact.

Rita's Mom
Age 42

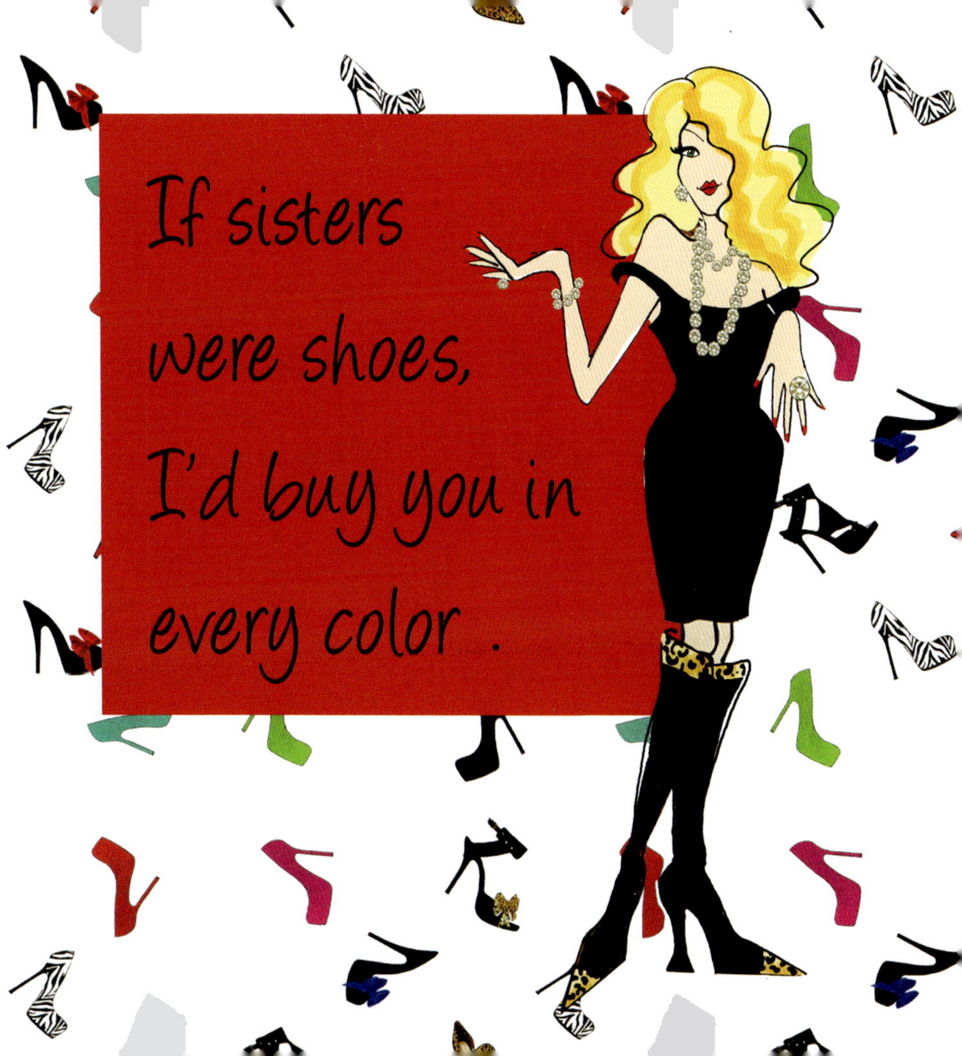
If sisters
were shoes,
I'd buy you in
every color .

Mother always said.. Walk softly and carry a big lipstick.

ON MAKEUP APPLICATION:

The trick is to put on enough makeup that you don't look like the walking dead, but not so much that you look like you belong on a street corner.

———

Alanna's Mom
Age 51

ON MARRIAGE:

Marriage is not that difficult, you just have to remember to compromise now and then and never forget that to men, sex is like air. They're gonna need it eventually.

———

Lisa's Mom
Age 53

Happily Married
with separate remotes

Some men are like babies, cute at first but full of crap.

ON MEN:

Men like to watch sports and then re-watch what they just saw in slow motion. And then the next day, they read about what they've already seen. This alone should tell you they have a very short attention span.

———

Carolyn's Mom
Age 51

ON PARENTING:

Don't be alarmed if one day
your child says they hate you.
You kids did it to me
all the time,
but I just pretended you
were dyslexic and had gotten
your words scrambled.

———

Melissa's Mom
Age 51

Help me,
Compliment me
or get the hell out of
my way

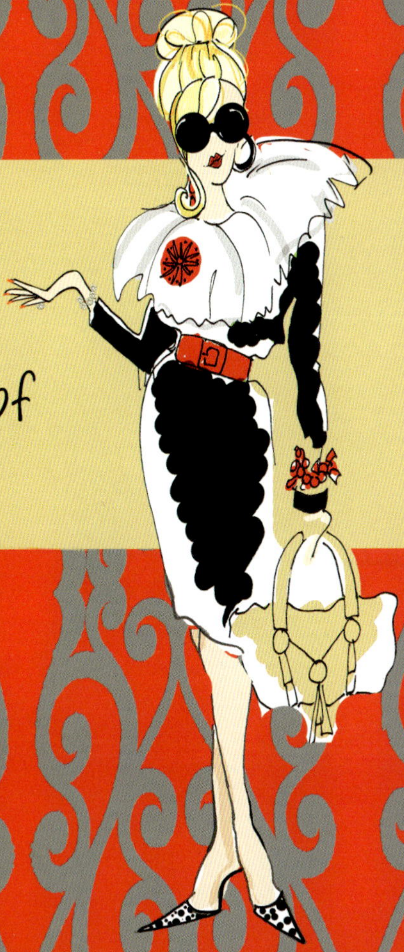

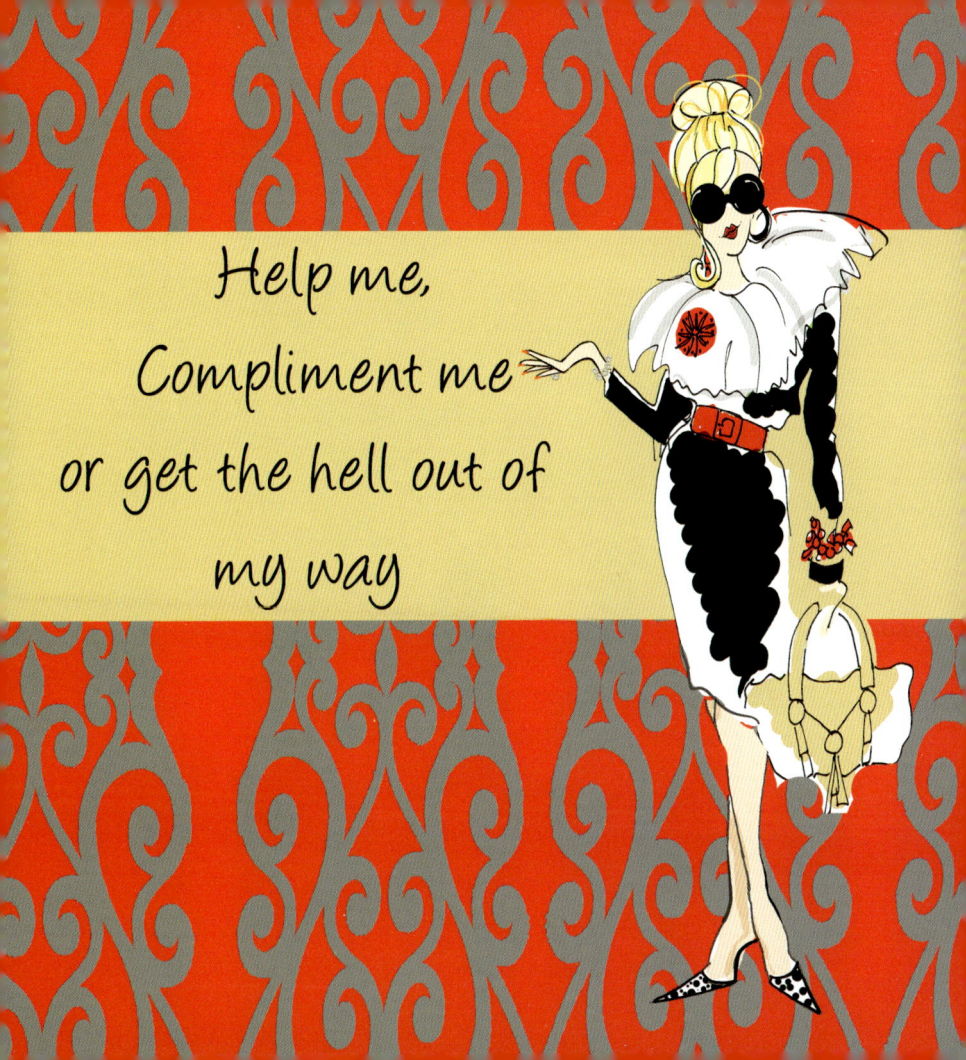

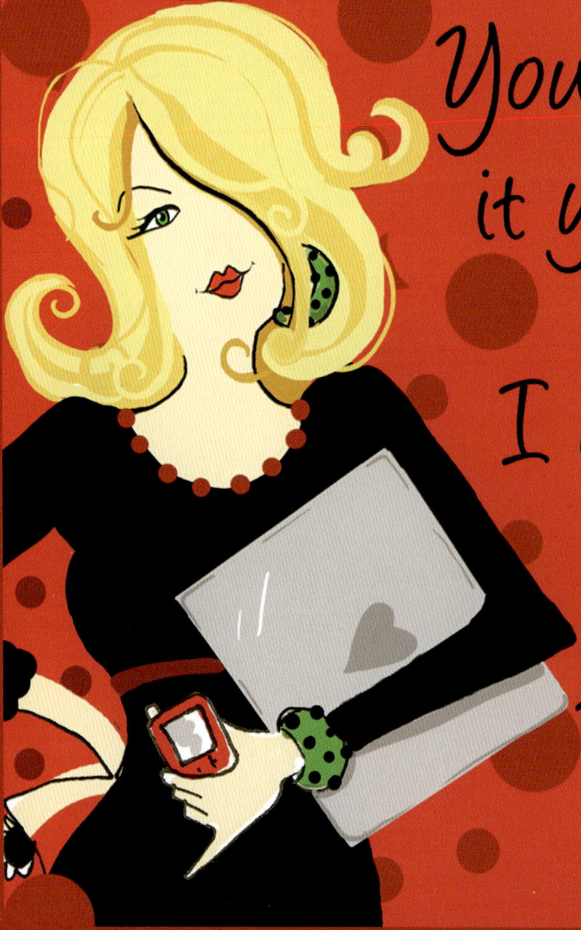

You can do
it yourself
or
I can do
it right
the first
time !

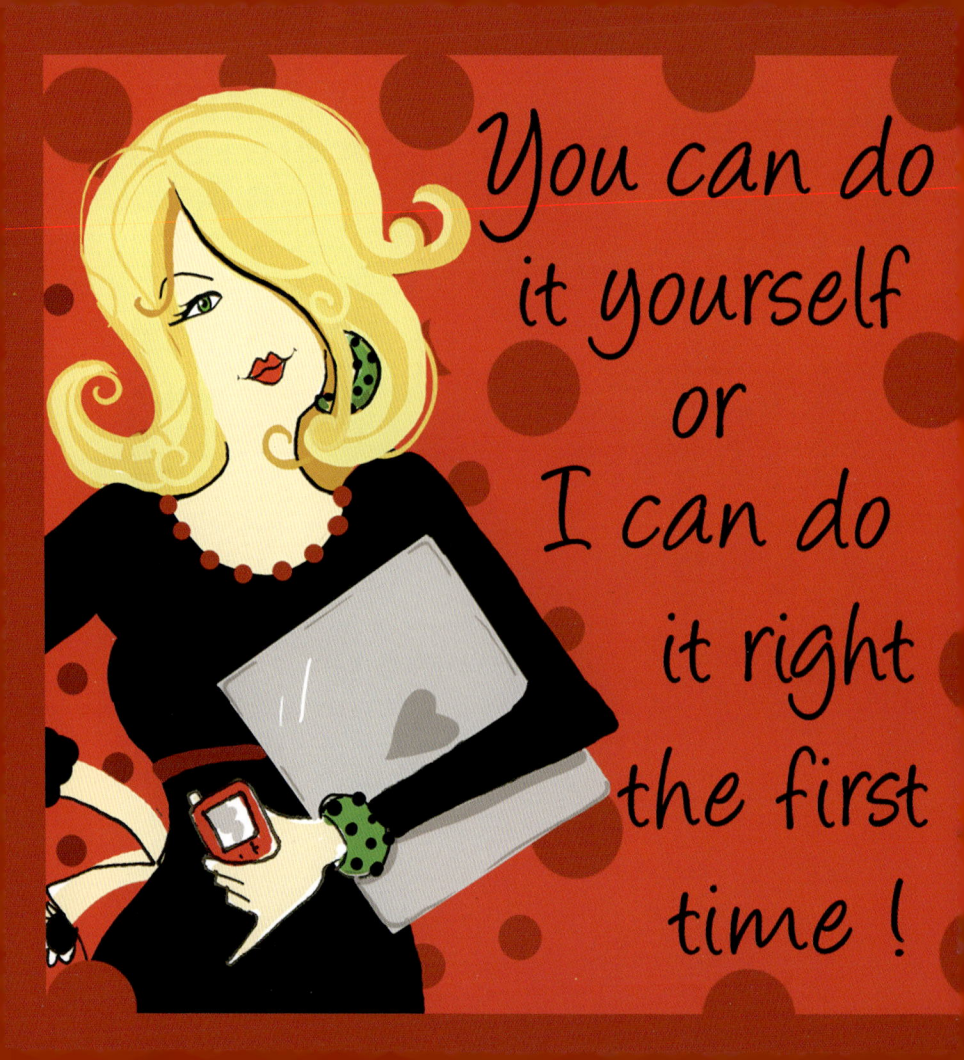

ON PLANNING:

I don't care what you
do with your life, it's your life.
But let me tell you something,
this is how it's going to be.

———

Charlie's Mom
Age 53

ON PRESENTS:

I don't want a card,
I don't need flowers. I want
one of you kids to
unload the damn dishwasher
without me having to
blow a gasket. Now that's
a present.

Carolyn's Mom
Age 47

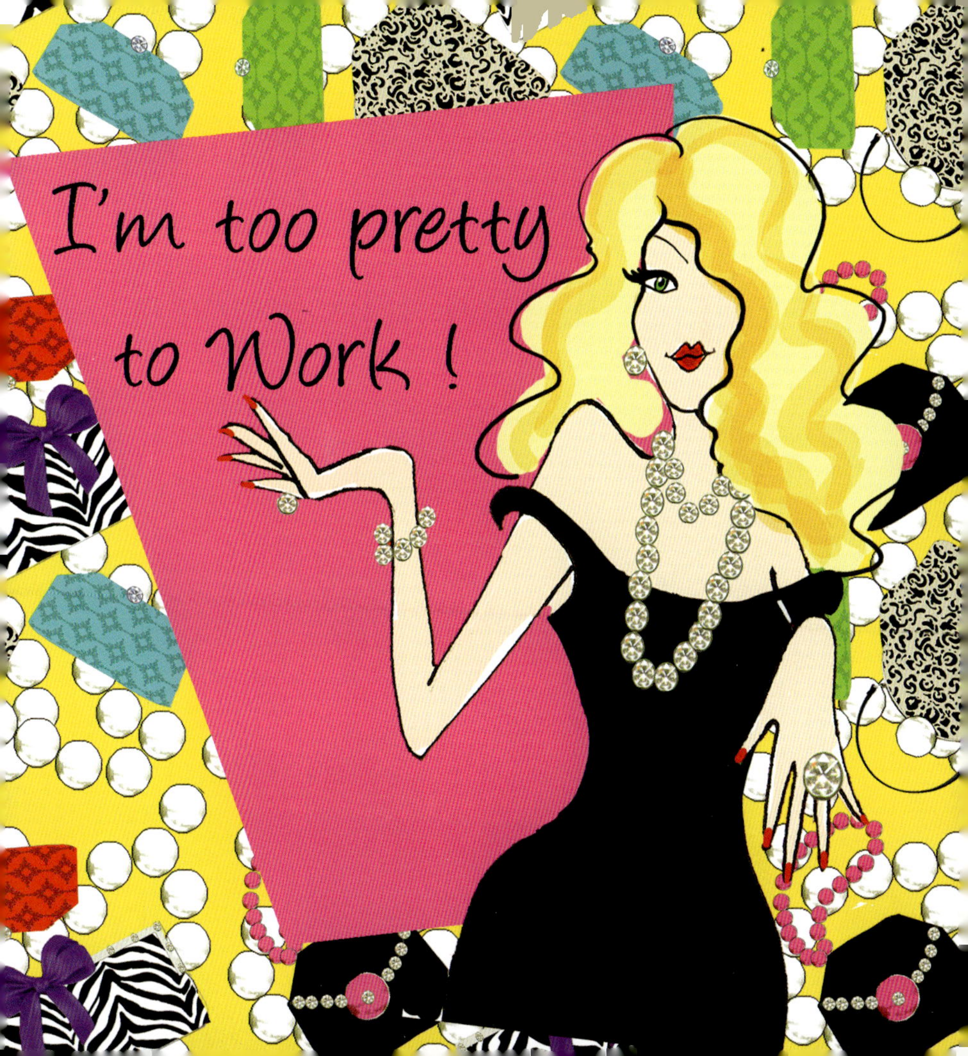
I'm too pretty
to Work !

Please wake us when the children have moved out.

ON SACRIFICE:

I could have used that money for my botox, but instead we bought you a new prom dress. Are you happy? I hope so because I can't see out of the left side of my droopy eyelid.

Sydney's Mom
Age 48

ON SCREWING UP:

I know I said that you could
never really screw up,
but that was a lie.
This is a royal mess
you've made.

―

Kara's Mom
Age 35

I didn't say it was your fault, I said I was going to blame you.

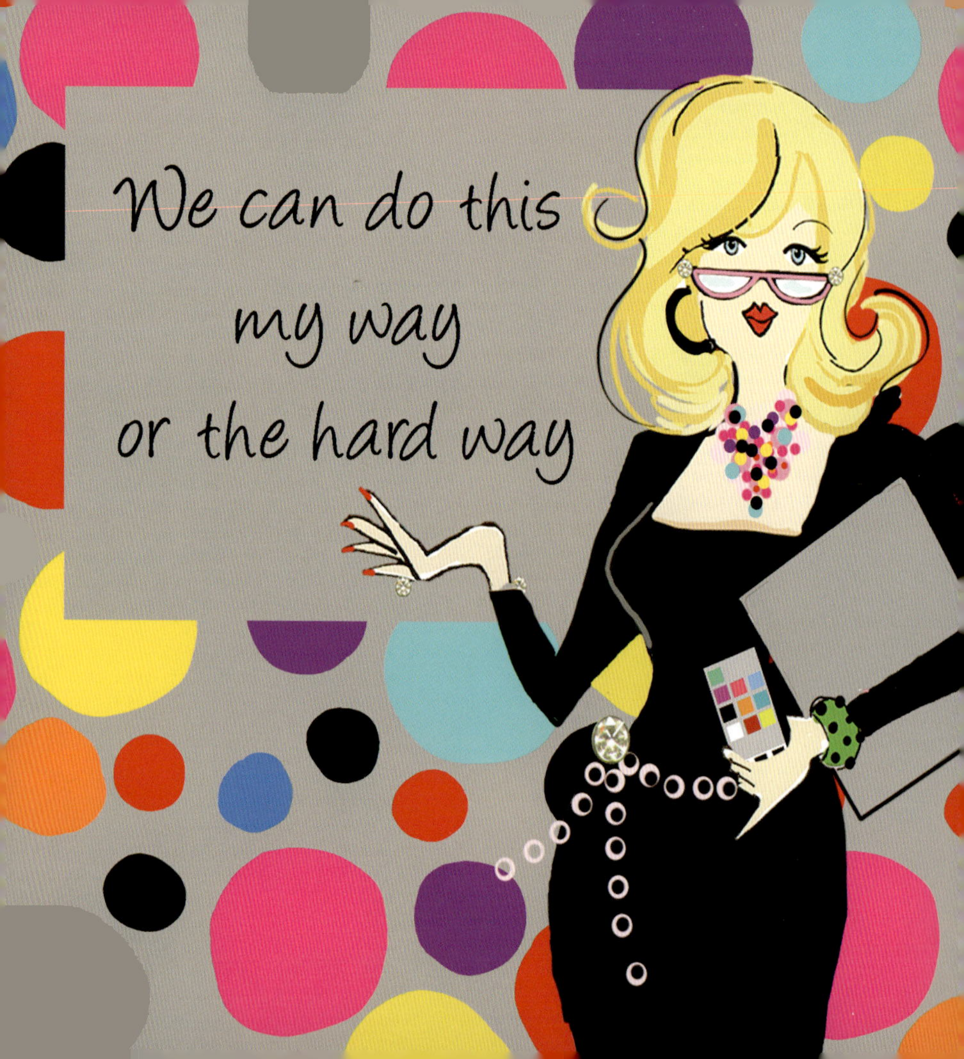
We can do this
my way
or the hard way

ON SENILITY:

Yeah that's right, I am old.
Old enough to take away
your cell phone and
forget exactly
where I put it.

———

Dana's Mom
Age 49

ON SHOES:

Men don't understand how we can have so many shoes for just two feet! They'll never understand it, so it's best to just buy the shoes anyway.

—

Jodi's Mom
Age 64

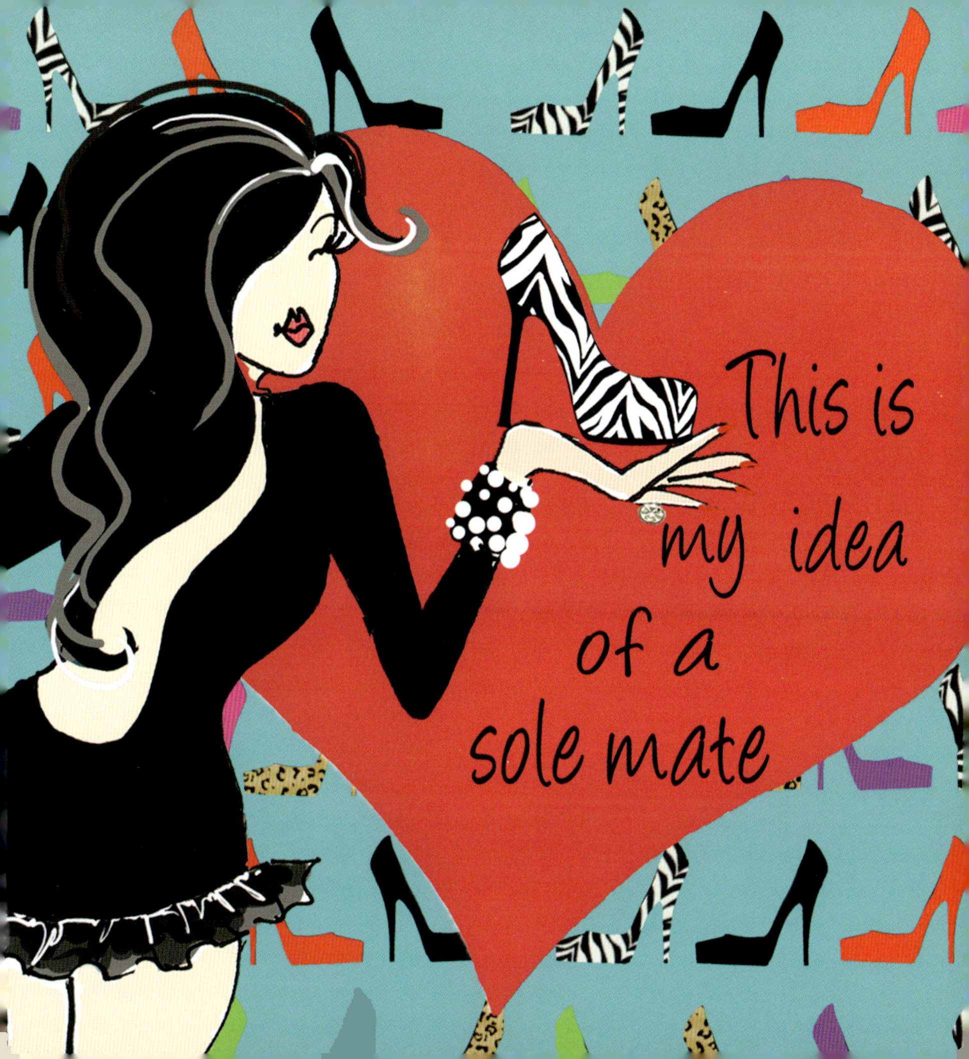
This is
my idea
of a
sole mate

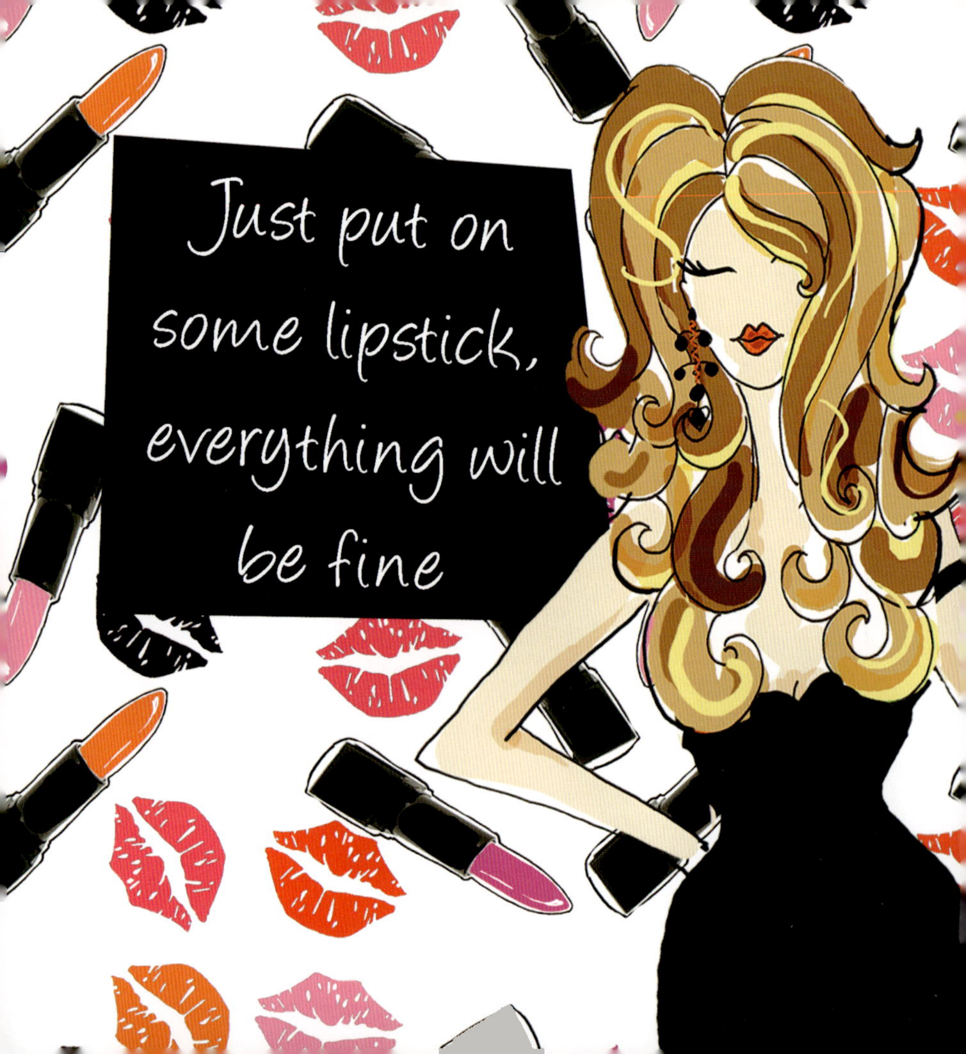
Just put on
some lipstick,
everything will
be fine

ON TELLING THE TRUTH:

Always, always, always tell the truth. Except when your girlfriend asks you if you love the bridesmaid dress she's picked out for you. Then it's okay to fib a little.

Donna's Mom
Age 49

ON WINE:

I don't want you drinking and doing shots.
Yes, I know I drink every night, but that's different.
That's just wine and that makes it okay.

Gayle's Mom
Age 51

I'll drink to that !

Don't make me De - Friend you !

ON YELLING:

Try not to yell at work or at home.
It makes you look
like the crazy one dear,
and most people go
the other way when
they see crazy coming.

Shelia's Mom
Age 49

Let's keep in touch!

In between cocktails, Artist Jodi Pedri and Writer Tonja Steel draw and write about all things fabulous. They were inspired to create this book from experiencing their own personal mamma drama! They reached out to their fan base and a flood of mother of the year stories emerged. Together, they have a singular mission: to create adorable and memorable gifts for Working Girls everywhere. You can follow along on their adventures at facebook.com/workinggirls or download their Free iPhone app: girl frames

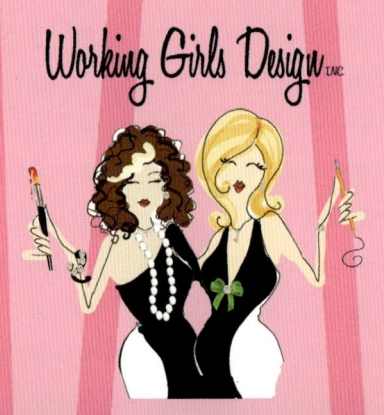

Working Girls Design, INC.